S C H O L A S T I C
LITERACY
PLACE®

Problem Patrol

Copyright acknowledgments and credits appear on page 144, which constitutes an extension of this copyright page.

Copyright © 2000 by Scholastic Inc.   All rights reserved   Printed in the U.S.A.

ISBN 0-439-06140-7

4 5 6 7 8 9 10   09   05 04 03 02 01 00

TABLE OF CONTENTS

PROBLEM PATROL

THEME
There are many kinds
of problems.

UNIT 2

Author/Illustrator
Taro Gomi

Ever since Taro Gomi was a little boy in Japan, he has always liked to make things. He started to draw as a way to express himself in pictures. In <u>Who Hid It?</u>, his colorful drawings speak a language of their own. Children all over the world can understand and enjoy them.

Who Hid It?
BY TARO GOMI

AWARD WINNER

 Who hid the glove?

Who hid the toothbrush?

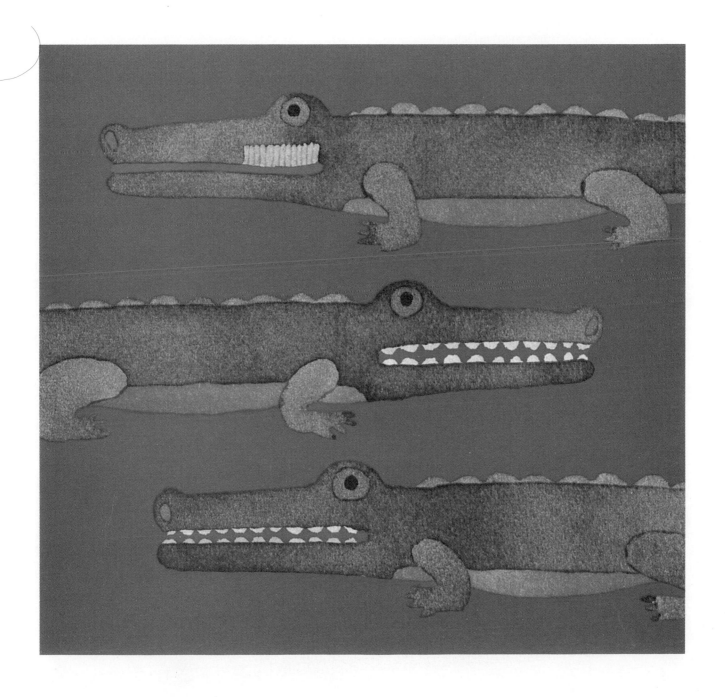

Who hid the sock?

Who hid the candles?

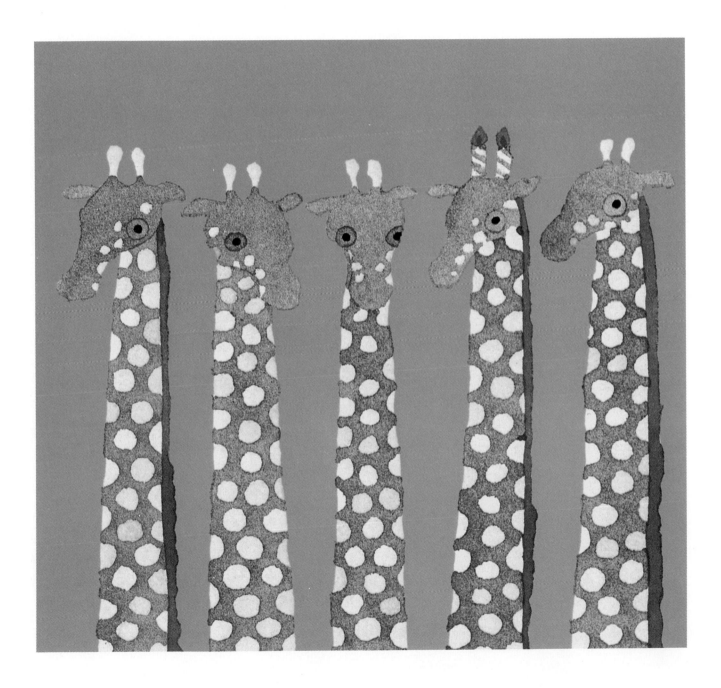

Who hid the cap?

Who hid the magnet?

Who hid the scooter?

Who hid the flag?

Who hid the pencils?

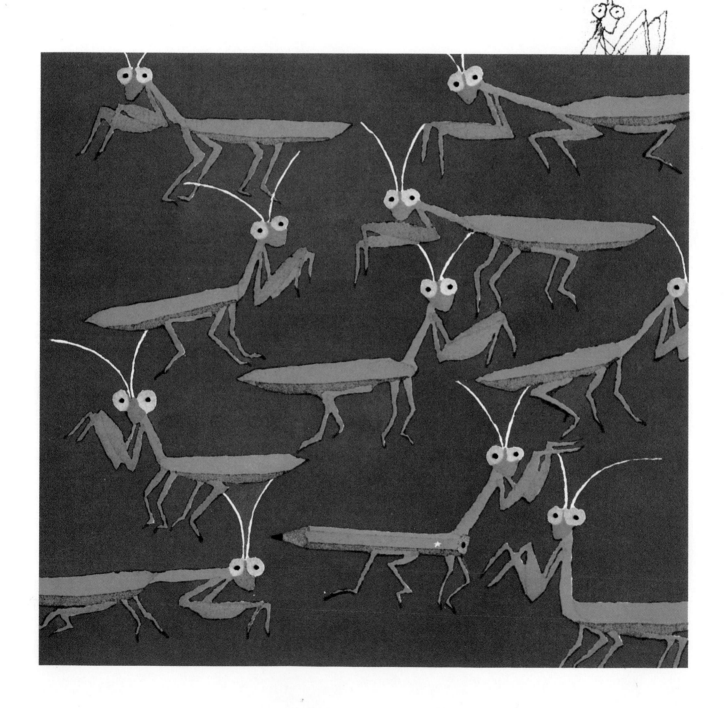

Who hid the fork and spoon?

What Is It?

by Cecilia Ávalos

illustrated by
Rosario Valderrama

Is it a pig?
No. It looks like a dinosaur.

But it is not!

Is it a fan?
No. It looks like a butterfly.

20

But it is not!

Is it a pan?
No. It looks like a balloon.

But it is not!

But it is not!

Look at the hill!
What is it?
It looks like a storm.

It is! Run!

I SPY

A Book of Picture Riddles

by Jean Marzollo

photographs by Walter Wick

Read Together!

I spy a rabbit, eleven bears in all,

A dog on a block, a seal on a ball;

One red bottle, one rubber band,

A wooden craftstick, and the letters in HAND.

Author
Mike Thaler

Author Mike Thaler says that writing a story is like painting a picture. Just like colors, he puts words down on paper. The words form stories that tell about his ideas, feelings, and humor. He especially likes jokes and riddles, and calls himself the "Riddle King."

Cinderquacker

a retelling of Cinderella

by Mike Thaler

illustrated by Dave Clegg

Chapter 1

Once there was a little duck.

Her name was Cinderquacker.

Cinderquacker had two mean sisters.

They made her mop the floor.
They made her fill the pots.
They made her wash the pans.

Her only friends were a cat and a rat—Don and Ron.

She sat on a mat with the cat and the rat.
They would sit lap to lap and all take a nap.
Cinderquacker would dream of the Prince.

The Prince was having a big dance.

But, he did not ask Cinderquacker to go to it.

Cinderquacker's sisters got to go.

"Off we go!" they said and they ran to the dance.

Cinderquacker was sad.
Then in came her Fairy Mom.

"Would you like to go to the dance?"
she asked.

"Yes, yes," said Cinderquacker.

So her Fairy Mom gave her wand a tap.
And pop . . . Cinderquacker had on a pretty dress.

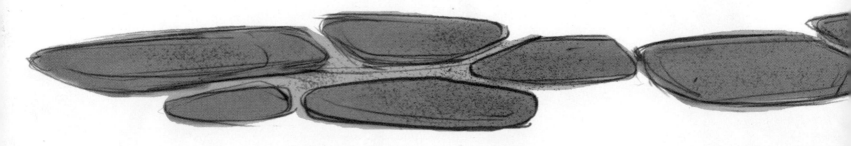

Then she gave her wand another tap.
And pop . . . Don turned into a van.
Ron turned into a man to drive the van.

Then she gave her wand another tap.
And pop . . . Don turned into a van.
Ron turned into a man to drive the van.

Cinderquacker got in and off they went.

Chapter 2

At the dance, Cinderquacker ran up to the Prince.

"I like you," she said. "Let's dance."

And they did, until the big clock hit twelve!

"I have to go," said Cinderquacker.

Then she ran out the door.
As she ran, Cinderquacker
stopped to toss off her shoe.

"I will find the foot to fit this shoe,"
said the Prince.

All the birds ran to put it on.

Ram! It did not fit.

Jam! It did not fit.

Hop! It did not fit.

Pop! It did not fit.

47

Then the Prince came to Cinderquacker's house.

"Will you put this shoe on?" he asked.

"It fits!" yelled the Prince.

He gave Cinderquacker a big kiss on the bill.

"You fit the bill," said Cinderquacker.

Then they ran off
and lived happily ever after.

The End

Higglety, Pigglety, Pop

by Mother Goose

illustrated by Mary Lynn Carson

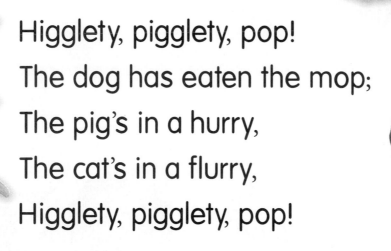

Higglety, pigglety, pop!
The dog has eaten the mop;
The pig's in a hurry,
The cat's in a flurry,
Higglety, pigglety, pop!

Authors
Alma Flor Ada and F. Isabel Campoy

Author team Alma Flor Ada and F. Isabel Campoy say that writing can give us the power to solve problems. All it takes is a pencil and paper, and we can change or create things to be just the way we like them!

The Picnic

written by Alma Flor Ada and F. Isabel Campoy
illustrated by Susanna Natti

Part 1

Kim: What a hot day!

Jim: Is the fan on?

Mom: The fan is on!

Bob: It's hot!

Dog: Yip! Yap! Yip!

Jill: Terremoto is very hot!

Mom: I have an idea.
Let's have a picnic.
We can sit where it is cool and eat lunch.

Jim and Bob: Let's do it!

Dog: Yip! Yap! Yip!

Jill: Terremoto likes picnics.

Kim: Let's go to the park.
We can sit on the hill.

Jim: Let's go to the lake.
I have a map.

Dog: Yip! Yap! Yip!

Jill: Terremoto wants to go to the beach.
He likes to play in the sand.

Kim: Here is my mitt.

Jim: Here is my bat.

Bob: Here is my cap.

Dog: Yip! Yap! Yip!

All: Where is the ball, Terremoto?

61

Mom: What can we have at the picnic?

Bob: I like bread and jam.

Jim: I like cheese and ham.

Mom: We can have bread and jam,
cheese and ham, and . . .

Dog: Yip! Yap! Yip!

Jill: Hot dogs! Terremoto wants hot dogs.

Narrator: Four hungry children, a big picnic basket, a Mom, and a dog, are all in a van on the way to a picnic on a hot, hot day.

All: Off we go!

Part 2

Kim: At last, we are at the park!

Bob: Can we sit here?

Jim: It looks like a good spot for a picnic.

Mom: Let's have a picnic!

Dog: Yip! Yap! Yip!

Jill: Where is Terremoto?

Jim: Look over there!

67

Jim: Pigeons here! Pigeons there!
There are pigeons everywhere!

Jill: This is not a good spot for a picnic.

Mom: Let the pigeons have the bread.
Let the pigeons have a picnic here.
We will go to the lake.

Jim: At last, we are at the lake!

Bob: Can we sit here?

Kim: It looks like a good spot
for a picnic.

Mom: Let's have a picnic!

Dog: Yip! Yap! Yip!

Jill: Please pass the jam.

Jim: Look at the ants!

Bob: There are ants on my pants!

Kim: Ants here! Ants there! Ants everywhere!

Mom: This is not a good spot for a picnic.
Let the ants have the jam.
Let the ants have a picnic here.
We will go to the beach.

Jill: At last, we are at the beach!

Bob: Can we sit here?

Jim: It looks like a good spot for a picnic.

Mom: Let's have a picnic!

Dog: Yip! Yap! Yip!

Kim: Pass the ham and cheese, please.

Bob: I see a seagull!

Jill: Seagulls here! Seagulls there! Seagulls . . .

Dog: Yip! Yap! Yip!

Mom: This is not a good spot for a picnic.
Let the seagulls have the ham and cheese.
Let the seagulls have a picnic here.
Let's all go for a swim!

73

All: TERREMOTO!

Jill: Terremoto likes hot dogs.

Narrator: Four hungry children, an empty picnic basket, a Mom, and a dog, are all in a van on the way to get ice cream on a hot, hot day.

All: Hooray!

Families in Art

Sunday Afternoon on the Island of La Grande Jatte, Georges Seurat

Many artists have shown families at home and at play.

The Family, Marisol

Tar Beach (Woman on a Beach Series 1), Faith Ringgold

📖 Read Together!

Dr. Fay Vittetoe
Veterinarian

All day long Fay Vittetoe is busy solving animal problems. See how she helps animals stay healthy.

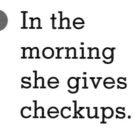

● In the morning she gives checkups.

● In the afternoon she answers questions.

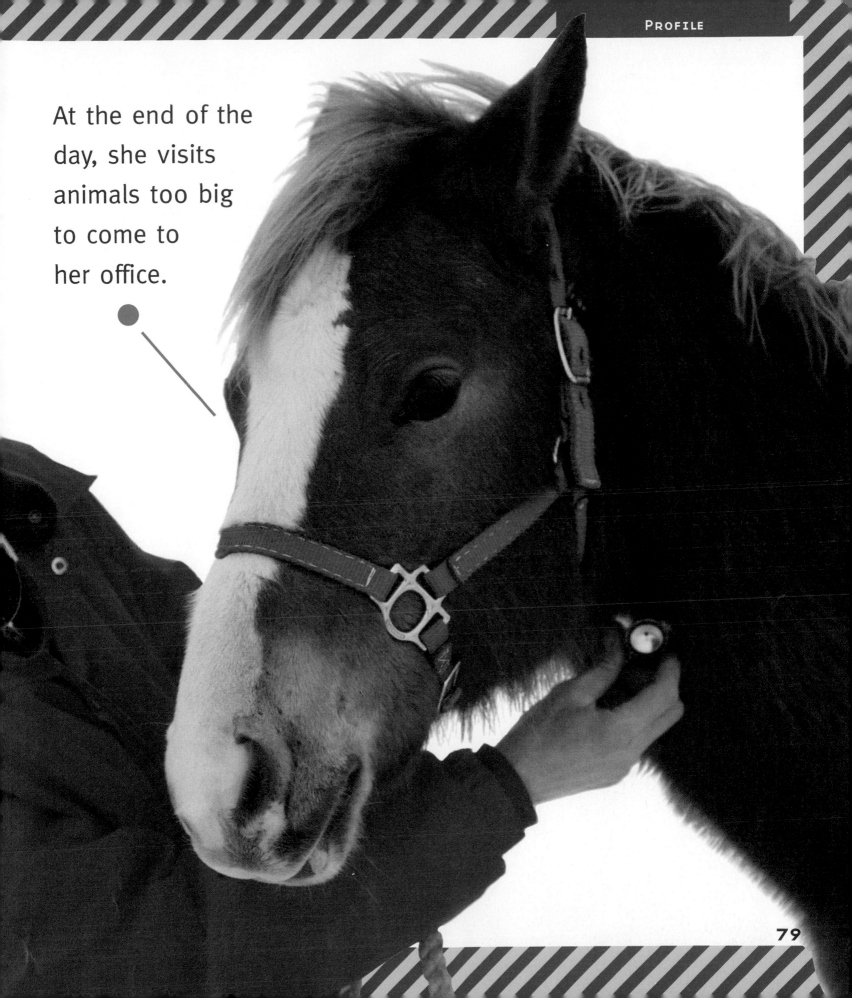

At the end of the day, she visits animals too big to come to her office.

What Is In the Egg?

By Su Wong

What is in the egg?

It is a baby snake.
It will slip out of the egg.

What is in the egg?

It is a baby chicken.
It will run in the grass.

What is in the egg?

It is a baby fish.
It will swim in the water.

What is in the egg?

It is a baby bird.
It will eat worms.

What is in the egg?

It is a baby penguin.
It will flap its wings.

What is in the egg?

It is a baby turtle.
It will live in its shell.

What is in the egg?

It is a baby alligator.
It will grow to be very big!

Author
Akimi Gibson

Akimi Gibson often uses
memories from her
childhood in her stories.
When she was growing up,
her father loved to listen
to jazz and musicians
like Dizzy Gillespie.
Skiddle-dee-do-dop!

That Sound?

written by Akimi Gibson
illustrated by Tammy Smith

NEWSSTAND

COFFEE HOUSE

Skiddle-dee-do-dop

"What's that?" said Liz.
"What can it be?
It sounds like jazz.
Let's go see."

Skiddle-dee-do-dop

Liz sat up.
She wants to know.
With a hip and a hop,
She's on the go.

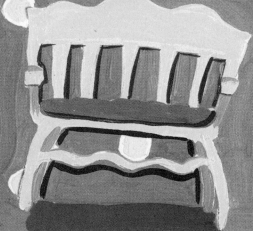

Skiddle-dee-do-dop

"Jim," said Liz.
"Do you hear that sound?
It sounds like jazz.
Let's look around."

Skiddle-dee-do-dop

Jim got up
With a hip and a hop.
And when he got up,
He did a little bop.

Skiddle-dee-do-dop

"I hear it too!"
Jim said with a shout.
"It's a jazz band.
Let's check it out."

Skiddle-dee-do-dop

102

FRUIT & FLOWERS

Skiddle-dee-do-dop

With a zip and a zap,
It was go, go, go!
They looked high,
But they didn't look low.

Skiddle-dee-do-dop

"Liz!" said Jim.
"We looked all around.
We can't find the band,
So let's sit down."

104

Liz looked at Jim.
She didn't want to stop.
Then she saw her dog.
He did a little bop.

Skiddle-dee-do-dop

Because right over there,
Down on the ground,
Was the bug jazz band,
Getting down!

Illustrator
John Sandford

John Sandford has illustrated many books for children, including Bumble Bear, The Dog Who Lost His Bob, and The Fox, the Bear, and the Fish. He hopes that his pictures come to life for the reader.

The

Good Bad Cat

by Nancy Antle   illustrated by John Sandford

The cat ran under the chair.

"Bad cat!"

The cat ran over the game.

"Bad cat!"

The cat jumped on the table.

"Bad cat!"

The cat saw a mouse.

So did everyone else.

The mouse ran under the chair,
over the game,
and across the table.

So did the cat.

The mouse ran out of the house.

The cat did not.

"Good cat!"

"Good cat!"

Did You See That Rabbit?

by Anne Schreiber

illustrated by Marcy Dunn Ramsey

Rabbits are fast.
They can hop, hop, hop.

128

Did you see that rabbit?
Where did he go?

Rabbits like plants.

They rip the tops.
Their teeth nip and chop.

Rabbits dig holes.

This rabbit ran into a hole.

She drops plants on top.
She hid the hole.

What is down in the hole?
Rabbit kits!

A rabbit can have lots of kits.

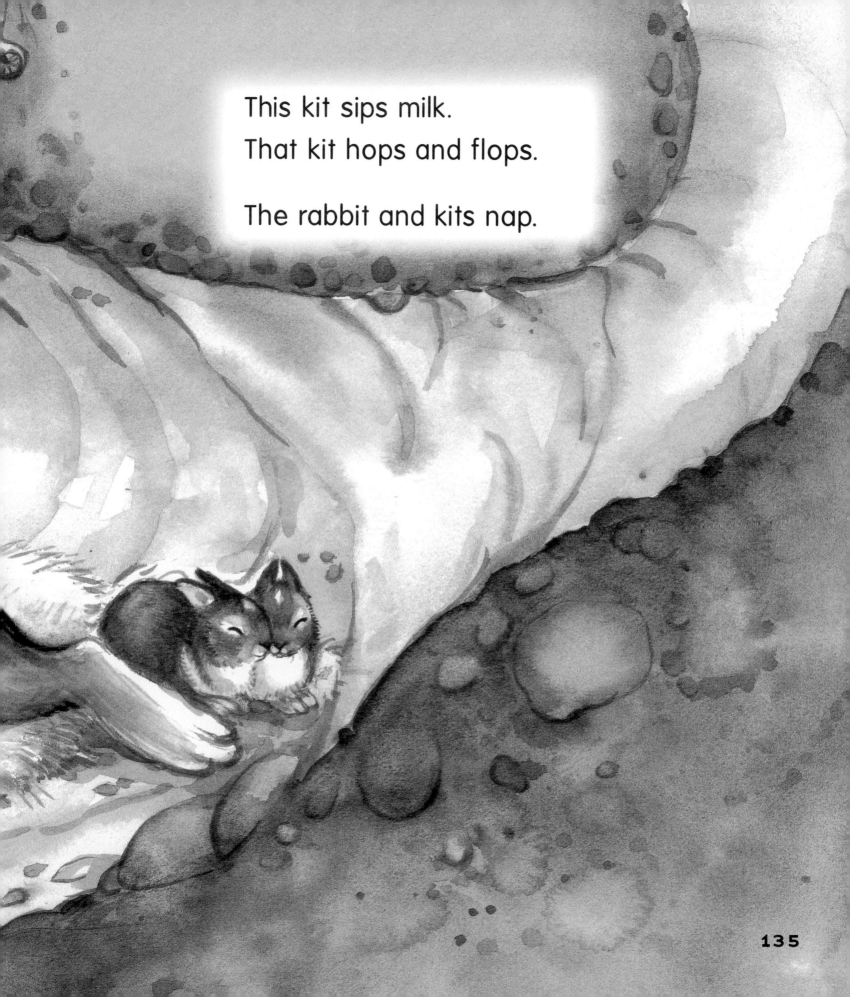

This kit sips milk.
That kit hops and flops.

The rabbit and kits nap.

Rabbits have to look out for the kits.
Do you see the rabbit up on the hill?
She stops and sits still.
She sniffs.

The rabbit and kits hop down—fast!

You can see rabbits out there.

You can see rabbits in here.

This rabbit will plop down
on your lap.
You can pet him.

Did you see that rabbit?
He likes you!

It Does Not Say Meow!

by Beatrice Schenk de Regniers
illustrated by Nancy Coffelt

It's glad when you're glad,
Sad when you're sad,
Has a head you can pat,
But it is not a cat.
(It does not say me-ow.)
And it doesn't say moo,
So it is not a cow.

It says woof or bow-wow.
Does that sound like a frog?
No! It's a . . .

Answer: dog

WORD LIST

Decodable Words

h

had	hill
ham	him
hand	hit
hat	hop
hid	hot

f

fan	flap
fast	flop
fill	frog
fit	sniffs

n

and	not
ants	on
band	pan
Don	pants
fan	picnic
hand	plants
in	ran
man	Ron
nap	van
nip	

c

can	cat
cap	picnic

i

big	kit
bill	mitt
did	nip
dig	picnic
fill	pig
fit	rip
hid	sips
hill	sit
him	slip
hip	sniffs
hit	swim
it	will
kiss	

b

bad	bill
band	bop
bat	rabbit

w

swim	will

j

jam	Jim
jazz	

z

jazz	zap
Liz	zip

p

bop	picnic
drops	pig
flap	plants
flops	plop
hip	pop
hop	pots
lap	rip
map	sips
mop	slip
nap	spot
nip	stops
pan	tap
pants	tops
pass	yap
pat	yip

d

and	drops
bad	glad
did	had
dig	hand
Don	sad

r

drops	rat
rabbit	rip
ram	Ron
ran	

High-Frequency Words

but	for	her	looks	over	there	who
did	have	here	no	she	they	with
down	he	let's	out	that	this	

143

Acknowledgments

Grateful acknowledgment is made to the following sources for permission to reprint from previously published material. The publisher has made diligent efforts to trace the ownership of all copyrighted material in this volume and believes that all necessary permissions have been secured. If any errors or omissions have inadvertently been made, proper corrections will gladly be made in future editions.

"Who Hid It?" from WHO HID IT? by Taro Gomi. Copyright © 1991 by Taro Gomi. Reprinted by permission of The Millbrook Press Inc., Brookfield, CT.

"I Spy: A Book of Picture Riddles" from I SPY: A BOOK OF PICTURE RIDDLES, photographs by Walter Wick, riddles by Jean Marzollo. Text copyright © 1992 by Jean Marzollo. Illustrations and photography copyright © 1992 by Walter Wick. Reprinted by permission of Scholastic Inc.

"The Good Bad Cat" from THE GOOD BAD CAT by Nancy Antle, illustrated by John Sandford. Copyright © 1996 by School Zone® Publishing Company. Reprinted by permission of School Zone® Publishing Company.

"It Does Not Say Meow" from IT DOES NOT SAY MEOW AND OTHER ANIMAL RIDDLE RHYMES. Text copyright © 1972 by Beatrice Schenk de Regniers. Reprinted by permission of Clarion Books/Houghton Mifflin Company. All rights reserved.

"Did You See That Rabbit?" from DID YOU SEE THAT RABBIT? by Anne Schreiber, illustrated by Marcy Dunn Ramsey. Copyright © 1998 by Scholastic Inc. Reprinted by permission of Scholastic Inc.

Photography and Illustration Credits

Photos: p. 30, Courtesy Mike Thaler; p. 54, Courtesy Alma Flor Ada & F. Isabel Campoy; pp. 76, *Sunday Afternoon on the Island of La Grande Jatte* (1884–1886) by George Seurat. The Art Institute of Chicago. Helen Bartlett Memorial Collection/The Bridgeman Art Library; pp. 77, *Tar Beach (Woman on a Beach Series #1)* (1988) by Faith Ringgold. Solomon R. Guggenheim Museum, New York; pp. 77, *The Family* (1962) by MARISOL (Marisol Escobar The Museum of Modern Art, New York. Advisory Committee Fund. Photograph © 1998 The Museum of Modern Art, New York. Marisol licensed by VAGA, NY. pp. 78–79, 78ml, 78bl, 79, Jim Heemstra for Scholastic Inc.; p. 80, © Wayne Lankinen/Bruce Coleman; p. 81, © J. H. Robinson/Animals Animals; p. 82, © J. H. Robinson/Photo Researchers, Inc.; p. 83, © G.I. Bernard/Animals Animals; p. 84, © S.J. Kraseman/Peter Arnold, Inc.; p. 85, © Dwight Kuhn; p. 86, © Mark Stouffer/ Animals Animals; p. 87, © D. Cavagnaro/ Visuals Unlimited; p. 88, © John Shaw/ Tom Stack & Associates; p. 89, © Laura Riley/ Bruce Coleman, Inc.; p. 90, © Robert W. Hernandez/Photo Researchers; p. 91, © E.R. Degginger/Photo Researchers, Inc.; p.92, © Zig Leszczynski/Animals Animals; p. 93, © G. Perkins, Dale Jackson/Visuals Unlimited; p. 94, © Wendell Metzen/ Bruce Coleman; p. 95, © Robb Helfrick/ The Picture Cube; p. 96, Courtesy Akimi Gibson; p. 108, Courtesy John Sandford.

Cover: Dave Clegg for Scholastic Inc.

Illustrations: pp. 2–3: Dave Clegg for Scholastic Inc. pp.30–51: Dave Clegg for Scholastic Inc. pp. 52–53: Mary Lynn Carson for Scholastic Inc. pp. 54–75: Susanna Natti for Scholastic Inc. pp. 96–107: Tammy Smith for Scholastic Inc. p. 142: Nancy Coffelt for Scholastic Inc.

Illustrated Author Photos: pp. 4, 30, 54, 96, 108: Gabe DiFiore for Scholastic Inc.